FOR ANNIE MARTIN
WHO BELIEVED

"SPIRIT OF MY SILENCE I CAN HEAR YOU."

SUFJAN STEVENS

"IF YOU DON'T KNOW WHERE YOU'RE GOING, ANY ROAD WILL TAKE YOU THERE."

GEORGE HARRISON

I WANT TO BE ONCE

POEMS BY M. L. LIEBLER

WAYNE STATE UNIVERSITY PRESS
DETROIT

20 19 18 17 16 5 4 3 2 1

Library of Congress Control Number: 2015956225

ISBN 978-0-8143-4202-2 (paperback)
ISBN 978-0-8143-4203-9 (ebook)

Publication of this book was made possible by a generous gift from The Meijer Foundation. Additional support provided by the Michigan Council for Arts and Cultural Affairs and the National Endowment for the Arts.

Designed and typeset by Bryce Schimanski
Composed in Adobe Caslon Pro, Trade Gothic and Orator

I WANT TO BE ONCE

MADE IN MICHIGAN WRITERS SERIES

A complete listing of the books in this series can be found online at wsupress.wayne.edu

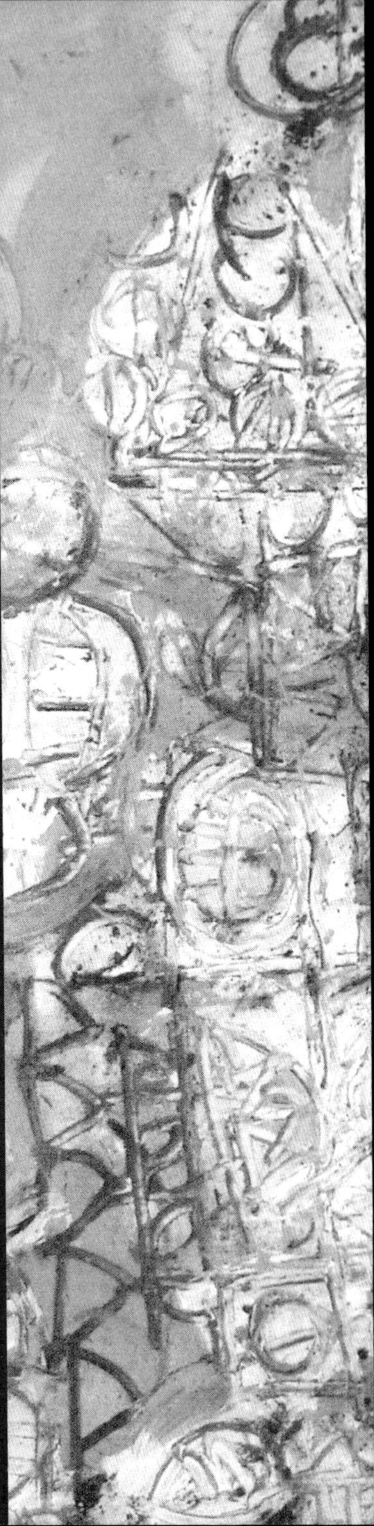

ADVANCE PRAISE FOR

I WANT TO BE ONCE

"You are hereby warned to take the cover of this book, open it, and hold on. This collection of poems is full of lavish disrespect at a time when wealth has never been more respected. Liebler's new poems are brilliant, magnificent, and transcending."

—Thylias Moss, MacArthur Fellowship recipient and award-winning American poet

"From the factories of Detroit to the deserts of Kandahar to the streets of Liverpool, M. L. Liebler brings a true voice of the American 60s—still pure with peace and love, still speaking in the lexicon of spirit and soul. And sure, Liebler takes us into the dark: 'Last night / I was awake / Counting fish / Inside my blood.' He knows the private and public war, he wants to redesign America. In this book, he proves the existence of God: 'Watermelon, / Beatles, / And the Infield Fly Rule.' Liebler is the real thing—buy this book!"

—Jan Beatty, author of *The Switching/Yard*

"M. L. Liebler is the poet laureate of America's working class. The collection he has assembled rings out with truth, intensity, and love. In a world full of despair, it is comforting to have writers so gifted and generous singing our song of rebellion and hope. This book is the kind of spark we need these days—a rich, intense, and inspiring collection."

—Michael Moore, Oscar winner and best-selling author

"In the growing M. L. Liebler world—peace, gentleness, self-understanding, all alight alongside the angry bull's-eye lances he throws. Beautiful!"

—Michael McClure, American Beat Legend

"M. L. Liebler is a fine poet. I know that his work, related to that of the U.S. greats and the less classic but highly idiosyncratic British poets, is very much his own. It simultaneously celebrates Liverpool and mourns for lost America and Americans. His poems always communicate, never intellectualize, and are not afraid of sentiment. M. L.'s compassion for this world ranges from Detroit to Afghanistan, and it clearly stems from his nurturing working-class roots. His combination of the normal and the extraordinary never fails to hit the spot. He is a genuine human being and poet."

—Pete Brown, poet and musician (former lyricist for Cream)

"These poems have tenderness, grief, loss, love, memory, history. They have workers' struggles and the hint and hope of revolution around the bend. The poet goes to war in these poems, and the poet claims the radiance that shines 'underneath / the shadow,' a radiance that 'dances right through sorrow.' Read these poems and find that radiance yourself."

—Minnie Bruce Pratt, winner of the
Academy of American Poets' James Laughlin Award

"The poems in *I Want to Be Once* are vibrant with M. L. Liebler's attempt to tie together all the threads of his Detroit factory grandparents, his fishing in Michigan rivers, Cass Corridor Arts memories, his adoration of languages fueled by travel, and in fact the politics of everyday life from which his vision of himself is made. These poems are honestly American and entirely without guile–rare, simple, truthful."

—Diane Wakoski, author of *Bay of Angels*

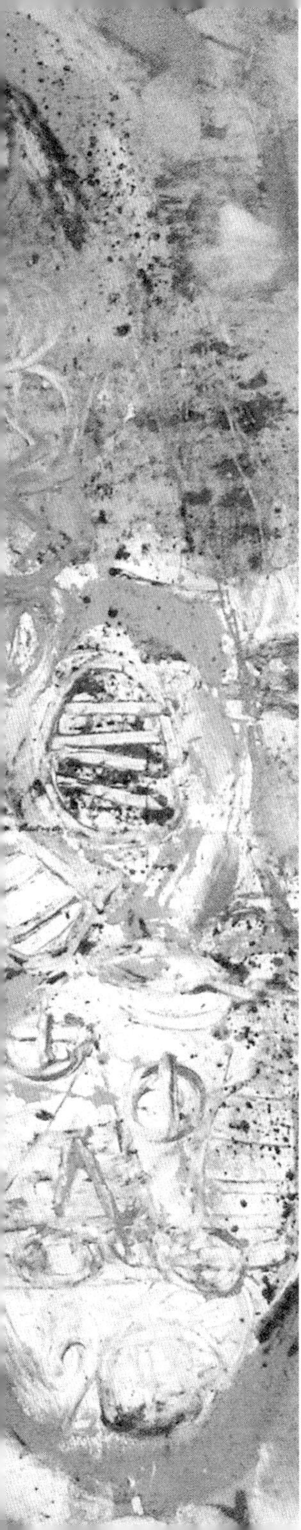

CONTENTS

PART 1 AMERICAN LIFE 1

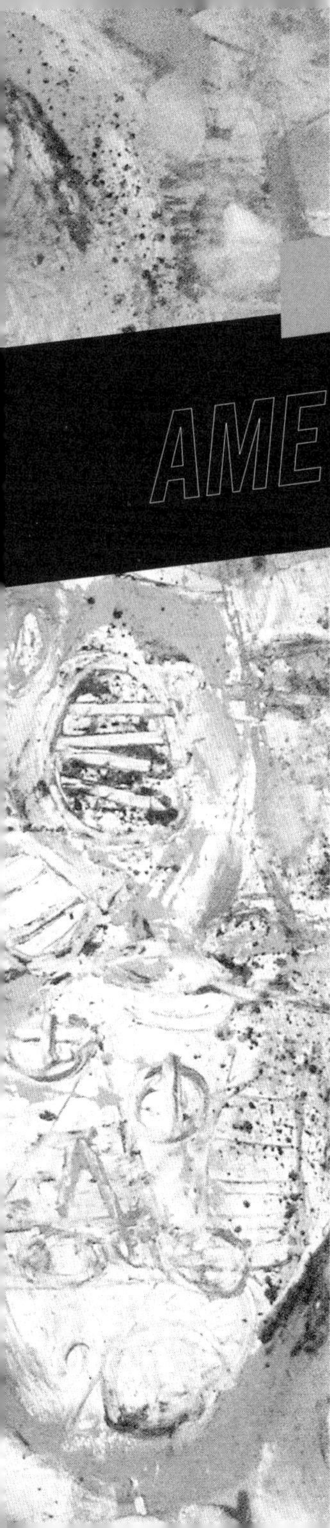

PART 1

AMERICAN LIFE

"I HEAR AMERICA SINGING,
THE VARIED CAROLS. . . .
EACH SINGING WHAT BELONGS
TO HIM OR HER AND TO
NONE ELSE."

WALT WHITMAN

UNDERNEATH MY AMERICAN FACE

Gramps, through all the years of layoffs
And callbacks, you worked in
The factory laboring endlessly
From your first day in Detroit until you retired
From the Dodge Main line 33 years later

Gramps, I sometimes wondered
What your life could possibly have been
With the exact same breakfast everyday at 5:30 a.m.:
Two fried eggs, bacon, toast, and coffee with condensed milk?
They say a man is
Measured by his soul.
Yours was dark and blue,
But I never understood much more
Of who you really were.

Gramps, who loved me more
Than any father loves a son.
In an old black & white photograph
You stand next to the neighbor's
New DeSoto with their small travel trailer.
I knew the only important thing to you
Was the sweet, dedicated woman
Whom you loved for over 50 years.

Gramps, you were always
The one I admired—
As you lived exactly what you believed:
Hard work, a paycheck,
And an occasional, small, treasured kiss.

Gramps, you never needed much
Because you knew,
As I am learning now,
It was never
About you. How silent
Your joy must have been
In your old battered Chrysler
That you drove back and forth
To work at the plant—

Like your own life
It was enough to get you from here to there,
With nothing at all waiting for you
At the end other than
A life
Well lived,
Complete.

I AM LOOKING FOR YOU NOW

FOR LAURA JEAN LIEBLER

Out from under the blanket of my life
I see your face
Alone and pale—my hero
Quiet and contemplative.
Your humor and grace
Alive in the night

Twin spirit of my youth.
The humor of a million laughs.
The strength of one hundred mothers.
My true friend in this family
Filled with hardship and pain.

I am looking for you now
In a past cluttered with broken promises,
Cobwebs of false witness
And the disrepair
Of things that once seemed possible
In the darkness of those summer nights.

Now, only the memories of small things remain:
The apple pie scent of grandma's kitchen,
Her floral housedress,
Gramp's calloused hand gentle on our hair.
The closeness we once shared.

I see you now waving through tears
Whispering that "We shall never be young again."
And I weep for all we once were
And for all that we will someday, soon, forget.

ONE OUNCE OF FORGIVENESS

FOR CARL ANIEL FOR ALL THOSE YEARS AGO

Alone in stillness I stood
Lost and broken by my grandmother's death.
In the old German cemetery
Where generations of my family lie
In the quiet earth cooled
By the summer shade trees.
Of this last season.
There you were again,
And my anger swelled
In the quiet of that afternoon sun
Where I could not find even
One ounce of forgiveness for you.

You, *drunken dumb song* artist, dope of my youth—
Long-haired, Indian headbanded hippie
With that same crooked smile.

Big, angel-headed, hipster
Who once pulled my dreams out
Of their sockets like cheap comedy hung
Out to dry in the linen breeze.

My grandmother gone now,
And I would have given up all
Hoping this day would never come.

And there you were again, floating
Up the big green cemetery hill
To hold me in my grief
And I almost forgiving
Myself for our past.

Filled with all
Stupid hope,
To slumber with the dead.

LAST NIGHT INSIDE MY BLOOD

Last night,
I was awake
Counting fish
Inside my blood.

All my life
Their gentle gills
Have brushed against
The blue walls
Of my dreams.

I should have removed
Their rusted hooks
From their tiny mouths
To free them in the moving
River of my blood,
But my soul could not let them go.

Last night—I tried, again,
To fall asleep counting
Each fish as it carried
        My life
                                        Up to the surface of grace.

THIS ATLANTIC LANGUAGE

"WHAT DOES NOT CHANGE / IS THE WILL TO CHANGE."
CHARLES OLSON

Up from the Atlantic,
—ancient words
Splash against broken rock.
High tide's wet letters
Pour down from
Blood in the moon.

Gloucester's clouds
Cover us with grayness.
Olson is at rest
In dreams that hang
Over Dog Town.

We weep for all
His words that we
Will never understand, spoken
In the tongue of salt
Understood only by the sea.

TREMBLING IN THE TEMPLE OF TEARS AT THE FEET OF BUDDHA

FOR RON ALLEN 1947–2010

After Allen Ginsberg

Who stood in the concrete fields and alleys of the Cass Corridor
With hope as wild as weeds in the everyday sidewalk cracks
Of Detroit. Deep pockets filled with poetry and Black Arts
Theater that could tell the truth of the future beyond our
hidden dreams.

Who understood and shared the phraseology of Donald Goines
A holy language—spun it into surrealistic parables
And laid them upon the dead bones of America's sunken chest.
A blood fever of poetry and ideas to bring new life to our city.

Hipster, futurist, teacher of the theater and poetry of backroom cafes Who knew the way to the heart was through song and word and not Through the lackluster academy and institutions that built themselves Upon their own self-pride while quickly diminishing and condemning The outside world of the streets into the skull cages of formalism.

Who knew the plight of the Bantu before America understood, And who held twenty-four-hour peace vigils sitting Shiva for freedom And equality in South Africa before the television and newspapers would Report the daily murders and violence in the broken houses of Soweto.

Who held, with tenderness, the grieving hands of Detroit mothers And grandmothers whose children had been lost to murder—killed By

other children in the mean streets of Detroit under vanishing skies
Of gray smoke, blue metal revolvers in the night.

Who put prayer in motion through Zen workshops and

Provoking koans that kept folks thinking of and dreaming for

New answers in the universe of ourselves beyond the here and now And beneath the heart and skin of God.

Who was aware of the brewing hatred in America's "post-racial" 21st century between city & suburb, black & white, rich and poor.

The invisible barriers that continue to kill the spirit and destroy
Who we are and what we should become.

Beautiful Buddha angel spirit who left Detroit to live
In warm sunshine of Los Angeles and to build
Another community of art and life in a distant city
Where pain was as real as the broken hearts
Of our Detroit. Where theater was not respected nor welcomed.

Where you took Zen meditation to the nth degree,
And beyond the long road that led you
Through Vietnam, Cass Corridor, LA, and back
To your Detroit—of community and grace.

You now, sweet Brother man, have returned to us
To live forever in the shade tress of our memories.
Eastside forever—reminding us always of who we all can
Be if we trust each other and heal and nurture
Each other back to life once again in the spirit of love and art.

I AM THE BROWN EARTH BURIED

I am the brown earth
Of Northern California
Asleep under a hot sun
Between almond trees
And avocado bushes.

I follow the wind
Deep into canyons
Inside my rectangle mind
Where northern autumns
Remind me of a million poems.

I call upon the rain
And the lowly winds
To bind every word
Of love that hides
Inside the heart.

LAST WORDS

FOR FARUQ Z. BEY

"You be at peace
With yourself."

His last words
To me while
Seated in the hot car
On another long hot
Summer Detroit day.

A soft kiss
Placed on both sides of your cheeks.
The last day we'd spend
Together after our many long
Rides through America.

Laughs, gossip, giggles, gigs
And more gigs for nearly
30 years in small rooms,
On festival stages, in
Broken urban classrooms.
We were grateful

To create, perform, and travel
Two "poets and a one-man band"
Together at home in this world.

It's your time now, brother man.
So you be at peace until
I come back to you to perform
Together, again, in eternity and light.

MAN ON THE MOON

When the first man
Landed, I was fifteen
And the world was at war.

I sat on our cement
Front porch of our brick
Ranch home, while
Grandpa drank a beer.

Grandma sat inside
That hot July eve on the plastic-
Covered couch, and she kept calling
Updates through the screened door.

"Mike, Vern, get in here!"
She yelled out.
"There's a man walking down
A bright white ladder onto the moon!"

We were listening to the ball game
On Grandpa's small transistor radio,
When a colorless, scratchy image
Of a man jumping

Off a grainy ladder onto the surface
Of a place we'd only seen
From our old bathroom window.
"Look at that, would ya?" she said.

My grandmother and grandfather
Only lived another ten years,
but on that hot July night
We were excited.

All of us huddled
On a small front porch
Watching a small black & white TV
Through a screened door marking
"One small step for man, and
one giant leap for mankind."

I WANT TO BE ONCE

When I pass
From this world to another,
I want to be greeted
By my old dog
Whom I loved more
Than much of my own life.

I want to, once again,
Feel her warm fur,
Kiss her tender ears
Pet that old tired pooch,
And run together, once
More, down the long corridors
Of memory.

ANOTHER AH SUNFLOWER!

When I return
To the garden,
I want to
Sing,
Shout,
And love
From the mud up
To the heavens.

I want to quietly
Grow into another
Sunflower and another
And another left to sway
In the wind and brush
Against the back
Fences of my soul.

JERICHO JERICHO

Written upon 10,000th Anniversary of the Great City of Jericho Upon the Request of the US State Department in Palestine

Jericho, your beauty glows outward
From the night stars
full throated
desert of antiquity. Alive
To all and as old as this world.

I still see your Mounts of Temptation
Rising high alongside the Jordan River's banks
And the Dead Sea's glistening soul
With God's angels aligned with yesterday's
Singing sun's warmth, rich, aridness
That soothes the awakening jackal's howl.

From the Bedouins outside your
Gates, grazing camels and sheep
Working the dried land,
Toiling in the everydayness of this life,
I know your true heart—
People alive upon this earth
In grace and bloom,
A desert flower of life and treasure.

Sweet city, O Jericho, where God first
Showed his face to bless this world.
Patient city where walls tumbled
Without lifting swords in anger.
Now, teach us the value
Of all your humbleness and wisdom.

Jericho, O Jericho you are our lasting
Memory. A desert flower,
Alive in the blessed dust
For over 10,000 years.

Your people have struggled through
Centuries of torment and anguish
To secure for us all a new dawn,
Built steady and solid upon
The ancient rocks of hope.

Jericho, where the words
Of your poets feed the many with
Daily bread. Where your past
Shows us the face of God
In His awesomeness and grace,
Beauty and tranquility
Your testament to the world is
A rich lesson of love and struggle
Brought forth from a vast
History of everlasting truth.

Jericho, now, we all march around you,
Not to tumble walls, but to pay homage.
Our simple prayer to an everlasting city.
Glow brightly now, sweet city
Under the eternal desert sun
Where God flows with the living waters
Deeply into the heart of this world.

MY GRANDMOTHER'S SWEET VOICE

Sailed through the wind
On clear summer days
And fell into my very young ears—
Manna from heaven.

I knew her voice,
Over and above all
Other mothers'.

Just a simple call
For dinner, for lunch—
A sweet sound at dusk
That led me home.

REVOLUTION

The days are long.
The future
A meandering
Old road
To nowhere.

I am tired, but I think
Something might be a comin'
Just around the bend,
Up ahead
Over yonder.

BLIND

Sometimes I wish I was
Walking down
Distant streets in lonely countries.
Just another stranger
Underneath my American mask.

Alone, I hide behind their
Old curtains and traditions:
In Siberia, in Palestine,
In places where pleasure is only
A rumor wrapped in a whisper—

A slow flame rising,
A swan's head dipping
In and out of a world
Of bad history, twisted up
With truth and emptiness.

LATE AUTUMN FIRE

A day will come
When I will have
Forgotten my own name,

And all the names
Of people I once loved
so dearly.

Names like hummingbirds
Working in the backyard
Of memory.

In the end,
Who will own
Our names?

PROOF

Once. Sitting
Alone with the stars

Gently lit, shining
Upon piles of autumn
Leaves—my damp past.

I do believe
That it can happen once
Every now and then.

Proof revealed, in the fleeting
Sliver of a quarter moon

TAKING WHAT ISN'T YOURS

You can never own it.
It will never belong to you.
You know with your whole heart
That it is wrong for you to keep it,
But worst—you know this is true.

Still, you persist. At first,
You tell yourself little lies.
Maybe you try hard to make
Yourself feel better with all that you
Have concocted to deceive in darkness.

But a morning will come,
Maybe even an early winter dusk,
And you will sit quietly alone, not even thinking
About the broken covenant of your own
Deceit. In fact, you will likely be

Very still and unsuspecting when
All the sins of this broken world
Will bring you a wave of pain, so restless
And wild that you will be washed far
Far away from the person you once were.

LIVERPOOL MORNING

My words moved
Upward in mist

Through the cold, brisk
Morning air on a street

In City Center Liverpool
On my way to Great

Charlotte Street and caught
A young Liverpudlian's ear

Who said, "I love the sound
Of the Americans. The words
Sound so rich to my ear."

LOST IN THE PAST, I DREAM

Into darkness I slip
My old warrior heart
Rattling like dice
In the dungeon of my chest.

I dream of Michael
Sitting alone on the shoreline
Of a sad lake, just another
Young boy kicked

Around in a world of blindness
And bitter hurt. He now wears a ring
From Belarus cut
From his father's old coins—

He keeps his dreams collected
In the quietness of his life
To remind himself of who
He was and the life that carried him

Further away from his
Eastern European roots
That now hang
Like chains of moss in his past.
Reminding him of his changing

Heart—an old country to where
He could never return,
So now he keeps a pen close
To write down all the stories
To place in the drifting
Folder of his history.

REREADING AMERICA

"AMERICA WAS NEVER AMERICA TO ME."
LANGSTON HUGHES

I want to reread America
I want to rewrite history as my own.
Shadows of ink on torn paper
Left lying by the side of a highway
Heading far away from here.

I want to re-create
America. With the same
Hard muscle of hurt
That America has always, painfully carved
Into the generous hearts of its people.

I want to redesign America
Make it fit like a puzzled star
Into its burnt flag soul.

IN THE WAITING ROOM

I sit not knowing
What is happening
On the other side
Of these four walls.

Is some sickness hidden
Underneath the paperwork,
Within the walls?

I notice my reflection
In that lone plate
Of glass. Leading myself
To a better place—

A wellness dream
        Beyond the glass, far
            from the dreaded diagnosis.

URBAN FARMING

I'm ain't goin back
To being no farmer
In Detroit, inventor of the middle class
The Arsenal of Democracy.

I don't want to order
My dungarees from no Sears catalog.
I don't ever want
To say, "How do?" to anyone.

I don't want to stop
And chat with local strangers,
While sucking on a toothpick
Drinking a Cokie Cola
In front of Floyd's Barbershop.

I don't want my grandchildren
Saying they can't play baseball
Until after they slop the hogs
Or after they seed the back 40.
I don't want my grandchildren
Yanking on no cow's udders for their milk.

I'm not going back
To those days when daylight
Saving was invented for more
Farming to get-ter done.
Screw that! Thank God I am
A Post-Industrial City Boy!

Some say Detroit needs to return

To "Urban Farming" to survive.
I ain't okay with shopping at Walmarts
And talkin' about the weather every
Five minutes. It just ain't okay
with me or my people.

We don't want to be
"Back on the Farm."
We just want our city back!

THE MIST SPIRIT OF EVERYTHING

Lying alone, very still
The cloud of childhood,
Masks my dreams
Inside its mist,
A spirit surrounding me.

In my youth, a fever
Of anxious flight
Kept taking me further
Away from the river
Of the living and into
The bright light of the unknown.

A radiance shone underneath
The shadow of my soul
That danced right through sorrow.

ELECTION

The first and last time
I voted with my grandfather,
We walked across a schoolyard,
Gentle mist touching our faces,
Under a gray November sky in 1972.

As we walked in silence
Toward the poll inside,
I asked nonchalantly,
"Are you going to vote
For George McGovern?"

In all my years,
I had never asked him
Who he voted for, but I did
On that Election Day
In a schoolyard in my hometown.

In the tormented
Final moments
Of a struggling campaign,
My mood lifted
When he turned to me
And in his quiet, but firm, voice
Said, "I'm voting Democratic!"

"Always remember, son,
We are working people.
We are Democrats.
This is what we do.
This is how we vote."

SITDOWN DETROIT 1937

On the factory roof
The night's blackness
Seems hungry and cold.

Below the workers
Tremble in the chill,
Heads hung low

Walking and thinking
Working and praying
This plant is closing

The men are
Staying inside
Until they get

One big union
for all. 1937. Detroit,
And this darkness will not hold.

There will be fairness
And equality
In due time.

These men have decided
For their children and families.
No more of this, sick and tired

Of being sick and tired.
They're sitting down right
Here and now.

They're taking over
This industry in spite
Of the police and bosses

Who have never respected
Who they are
Now, they can call

In their militia.
Ask their mayor
And their politicians

For help,
But these men
Ain't movin'

TO THE WAITING CAR WITH MR. SALINGER, MR. LENNON, ALICE & ME

"Bid thee farewell,"
John Lennon was
Once overheard to say
To a cashier
In New York City
At FAO Schwarz's,
When she asked when his next
Album would come out. He said,
"I've made my contribution
To society," and he slipped
Out to a waiting car on Fifth Avenue.

As Salinger said, "Enough of this world,"
And he slipped away to a house
On a mountain in the East.

And now, dear Alice Munro and I
Are deciding to move along
While we still can
move along.

We want to decide
When and what we will write.
Our final poems or stories, or
And when we will write no more.

So, this is
Our time,
and we're taking it—
Out the door with the door.

A POEM OF SERIOUS DOUBT AND WONDER

How many nights have I
Stayed awake lying in my suburban
Bed wondering when the end
Would sneak up upon my life
through the dreaded back door of death?

My beloved grandparents
Who cared for me
Who gave of themselves
Two old people stepping up
To change diapers, heat formula,
Nurture a young schoolboy
From Elvis to tying shoes
To waiting for the bus on cold
Mornings when I could write
My name in my morning breath
Sending it up to the skies.

Once as a little boy in pajamas
On a bed looking toward the night ceiling,
I saw a black ancient planet where I hoped
All the people I loved would live someday
FOREVER. The great beyond calling
My sweet grandmother
And grandfather
To surrender

So now I sit alone on a cold fall day in a place
Where I can be
Home in this world, but not of it.
I came into a broken world broken. I can't
Go back. I am moving forward
Into grayness. I have trimmed my lamps
As I walk toward a village beyond the sun.

HOPE

A sly thing.
It pokes its head out
From under
Tumbling sagebrush
Or up from the bottom
Of an old pond.

Other times
Hope slides past
Everyone who seeks it.
A slippery cloud of softness.

We'd all like to reach
Up and grab us some
And pull it snug to our hearts,
But hope is very sly thing.

UPON CHRIST'S ENTRY INTO LIVERPOOL

After My Beloved Liverpool Hero Poet Adrian Henri

"But All Will Be Well, and Every Kind of Thing Will Be Well."
Julian of Norwich
The banging drum,
The marching band,
Up Lime Street, signal
The holy holiday.

O ghost of youthful past,
Where bombs once smashed
Upon Mersey docks
Blackness, fire all
Smoke of war rising
Off the backs
Of the lonely and indigent,
Let all say, "Liverpool
Lives even after the rubble."

The stagnant puddles
Of standing water
Darken the alleys off Hope
Street—A testament
To the baptismal flow
From the blackened cathedral
Fonts that stand alone
At each end of a long block.
Bookends of faith
In a city burdened by time.

Rise O Liverpool

From your tortured sleep
Of the sea, from your
Weary neighborhoods.
Of post-industrial Toxteth.

Arise O sweet music
Your witness to all that is good
And lasting about Liverpool:
Yeah! Yeah! Yeah!
Secret chants from the deep
Dark caverns of Lazarus.

"Come forth from the cave
Of yourself where death has filled
The stones with the brutal
Loss of black salty water and lime.
Leave behind what can you can least
Forget. Leave behind

Stuart Sutcliffe's pain and angst.
Leave behind John Lennon's
Bleeding mother lying on Menlove Avenue.
Leave behind Brian Epstein's
Penny Lane homosexual shame.
Leave behind sweet, betrayed Casbah
And Mendips anger, Forthlin Road death.

Leave behind Mathew Street raising,
Leave behind Italian Beatle Boot
Lament. Leave behind rocking Mojo's,
Undertakers Searchers and the brokenness
Of the Big Three & Jimmy Campbell,

Poet Laureate of Liverpool streets.

Leave behind Melville's laudatory praises.
Leave behind the sweet notes
A Liverpool Oratorio. Leave behind
Butcher Cover madness, Ed Sullivan,
London Palladium screaming, and rusting
Yellow Submarine of Ringo's Dingle.

Let all the pain out to
Pour it all over and down from your
Ironsides and wooden docks into the Mersey.

Celebrate and call out now
To the happiness you have
Freely delivered to this world
In the sight and sound of God
And nature. Heal the broken
Dreamers—now as alive
As when they first heard "Love of the Loved"
Gently floating from a churchyard in Woolton
Near the graves of Father McKenzie,
George Toogood Smith and Eleanor Rigby.
Through the pines of St. Peter's Church

Let us again hear the goodness of mankind
Again to heal the human suffering of the dead
Foreign wars, race riot madness
And our own lack
Of faith and prayer.

O Come O Sweet Adrian to this
City. Open Liverpool

To empire beauty,
Sweet promises of its former self
To now be redeemed
By what you were and what you
Can now become—
Again
Again
And again.

ACROSS THESE LAWNS

The Poet Laureate Poem for St. Clair Shores 2005
Hanging in the St. Clair Shores Public Library

As a gentle breeze wafts through a summer afternoon
Crossing the green fields of Couchez Farm down toward
The water, we remember our city asleep by the Lake of St. Clair.

Once only a lonely Township of Erin on the water—
Later, a village and later still a city
Sitting in the backyard of Detroit.

My city eases itself along a shoreline dotted
With baseball field vacant lots, lakefront parks,
King trees in bloom, and full freedom

Place where we once fished through broken ice
In spring. Cold water flowing downwind from Memorial
Park in a parade of life to Eagle Pointe's shore and up

Past Blossom Heath and into the marinas of my youth.
I remember you fading ghosts of Jefferson Beach
Staggering through the fire in my childhood

Dreams—Sacred playground of the world's
Largest roller coaster, corn dogs,
Cotton candy and holy big band sounds

That enveloped twilight dancers in the breeze
From small gales that whipped the lake
Into tiny whitecaps that hung on like clouds

Above the fresh waters at 9 Mile Road.

Ah—the beautiful aromas and sights of those
Long years—where wind and waves danced together

Over deep county ditches and smooth frog ponds.
Sliding over ruts alongside old 12 Mile Road & Greater
Mack, and down the quiet streets of Ingleside-Grossedale
Park

My neighborhood of fish fly mornings,
Where we washed our sleep away
With the garden hoses of memory.

This is where we were born, and our
Parents the same. Now our children
Live here in this easy blend of nature and city

Along these lakeside streets filled
With hope—setting sail forward
Into the new century of life.

THE QUIET APPLE

Sits alone,
Quiet. A shadow
On a tabletop. Surrounded
By nothing. Glistening with rain.

Like rain on a still
Bough of a tree just before.

It falls
I want to snatch it

And bite into its soft skin,
Breaking open the juices

To flow down my innocent
Lips, widening like an open wound

A stinging cut
Sweet, fresh juice of change.

My appetite a small reminder
Of all my indiscretions.

PART 2

AMERICAN WAR

THE KANDAHAR BLUES: DUST & POETRY

The tanks left in dust
And wind. Fired up
Their guns—tested and ready
Shots smashing into bales
Of hay on the outer ring
Of a big stone airfield.
We moved slowly toward
The waiting poets.

They were expecting
An American to visit
To talk peace, poetry,
And liberation. With broken
English and subtle metaphors,
We understood the true
Meaning behind the words.

HOT HEAT JALALABAD

Today, we are going
To lose ourselves
In the Jalalabad moon.

I told the Pashto kids—
Think of our slow movement
Like an orange falling
From high up in a tall orchard

It hits the ground
And breaks wide open,
Seeds and all.

VACANT CHAIR

This is the new America
Just a broken neighborhood.

An empty house here,
A lost family there,

Twisted remains.
An explosion

That leaves nothing
Standing in its wake.

All we ever wanted
Was a little corner

Of this world to raise
Our families, and to praise our God,

To sing our songs,
But now—

Just an empty house here,
A broken dream there,

And a vacant chair.
Abandoned alongside a curb.

WINTER MEDITATION

Within a cool winter's
Meditation, crystals form
along the fine hairs of my mustache,
I taste the salty dew
Falling from yesterday's stars.

A bitterness in my mouth
As sad as the ocean.
Still, I'm drawn into its waters,
Deep below the surface tides
Colder than the blood in my heart.

The salt I taste now reminds me of
Every broken dream,
Every undiscovered truth,
Every distant shore
I've never reached.

I live filled
With sorrow for all
The things I've never said
As my soul crawls through
The desperation of the moon.

RESTREPO'S SHADOW

The helicopter landed
On a bed of rocks
At Finley-Shields,

Afghanistan. I pulled
My earplugs
Out, and jumped

Onto the ground.
Alive. I was in
The old Russian compound

Where it is rumored
That Osama Bin Laden
Stayed for a little R&R.

It is also rumored
That the drained pool,
Now a basketball court,

Was used for executions
By the Taliban, post USSR.
Two soldiers were shooting

Some hoops when I arrived.
My guide showed me
To my room and just past where

The Taliban fighters had tried
To crash the gate two days before.
A firefight left all of them

Dead. He pointed to all
The places they were killed.
"We got one there, there, and there And one little bastard was shot
And killed right there under
Your portable classroom."

KORENGAL VALLEY: CAMP RESTREPO

On a clear, warm night in Jalalabad,
I sat outside my hooch on an old Russian chair
Staring at the mountains receding into darkness.

My roommate walked out to admire the stars.
He told me to focus on the top of that mountain,
And he said, "Have you heard of Korengal?"

While I shouldn't know this word
Any more than my neighbor's name,
my students, or my "co-workers," I did.
I knew it was the area of the deadly Operation

Rock Avalanche, Camp Restrepo. I asked
If that indeed was "the place?"
"Yep. Some real bad shit over there, my brother."
In war zone contemplation, we both knew there was no
more

To say. We both started out over that mountain.
We both knew Death was just on the other side,
Down a slope. Taliban Country.

KANDAHAR MISSION BRIEFING

They brought me in quietly.
Sitting us all in a large half circle—
A chalkboard, a captain
And a mission leader.

"The mission is to take this poet into
City Center Kandahar tomorrow.
To get into the city,
We will take four MRAPs.

The leader will scout
The road ahead for IEDs.
The middle one will carry
The poet and a turret gunner.

The third and fourth vehicle will
Serve as lookouts and follow up.
If any of these vehicles hits
An IED, and if the vehicle doesn't

Tip, do not, under any circumstances,
Exit the vehicle. If the gunner
Is hit or killed, the poet must
Grab his legs like thus and hold on.

You must not let go of the gunner.
When we arrive at the outpost,
Soldiers in vehicles one, three
And Four will exit and search school grounds

For insurgents disguised as Taliban poets.

When the all clear is given, the poet
Will exit vehicle number two
With body armor, helmet, and first aid kit.

He will be surrounded by six soldiers.
Once the okay is given, soldiers
Will bring poet into building
Where the poet greets the director

And 34 male Kandahar poets and authors.
If room is not compromised,
Poet may take off his body
Armor. If scene seems dangerous

He must keep armor and helmet on at all times.
After talk, reading, and hummus, we must
Leave grounds ASAP. No lingering!"

FURTHER ON UP THE DUSTY AFGHAN ROAD

After our mission,
After handshakes, hugs
Inspirational words,

We all drove away.
I was then informed in the MRAP,
"That School Director will likely be executed

For collaborating with Americans.
His family too."
I was told

Not to concern myself
With that.

MOSTLY NOTHING HAPPENS

My hero war poet W. D. Ehrhart,
Served recognizance
In Vietnam in a war where
"mostly nothing happens."
But when it does happen,
Death is often close
behind. I did not
understand this until
I landed in Afghanistan.

Mostly nothing happened,
But there were moments
When I felt a jolt, heard a machine gun
And watched mortars fly,
Death waiting behind each explosion.

WIND, DESERT, DUST

Deep into the windy desert
The dust of Kandahar sticks
To clothes, skin.
Grit burrows into the soul.

I search for shade,
A small bruise to hide
From this terrible sun
Arising in the heat of war.

I am stranded
Alive in terrorism
Surrounded by everything
Dangerous. Here is a mean season

Where I feel as a young boy,
Trapped in a dream under
A blistering sun
Of war and rage.

OH! THAT ANTI-WAR JESUS AGAIN

FOR DOROTHY DAY

He made it all so simple then:
"He who lives
By the sword shall die

By the sword,"
And he healed

His enemy's
Wounded ear.

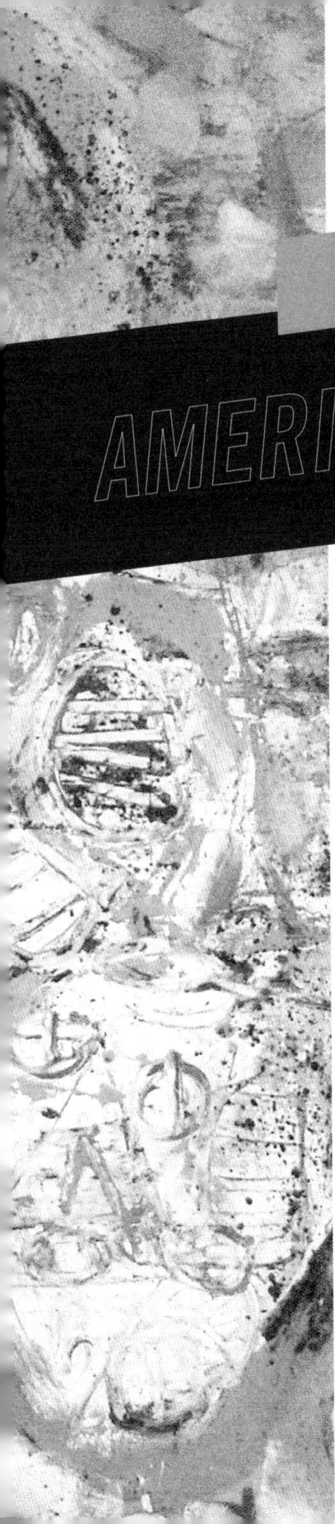

PART 3
AMERICAN PSALMS

"ALL THINGS CAN WAIT, BUT THE SEARCH FOR GOD MUST NEVER CEASE."

GEORGE HARRISON

AMERICAN PSALM: WHICH SIDE ARE YOU ON?

Remember that Syrian rebel
Cutting out a man's heart
And biting into it on live TV?

How about their murdering 7 POWs
By shooting them in the head
With their hands tied behind their backs?

If the US decides to meddle in Syria's civil war,
These are the people we'd be helping.

AMERICAN PSALM: PUBLIC RADIO

Wait, Wait,
No-Really,
I am serious
"Don't tell me!"

AMERICAN PSALM: THE HOODIE BLUES

If George Zimmerman had just told the truth
Florida would've saved the tens of thousands of dollars

It spent to sequester a suburban jury in a nice suburban
Hotel and supply them with Cracker Barrel
Dinners and a field trip to see the newest *Lone Ranger*
movie.

And old George would have lived happily
Ever after in a prison cell for life for murdering
A teenager with a bag of candy—Kemosabe.

AMERICAN PSALM: WHAT'S ALL THIS PUSSY RIOT?

This is not the same pussy
Those guys at football
Tailgate parties
Are excited about.

AMERICAN PSALM: TEA PARTY ANYONE?

Think about this!
You're aspiring to
Overthrow a major superpower
That has many fighter planes
Warships, bombs, and guns.
They have way more
Firepower than you have sense.
Come on, Dudes.
Really?

AMERICAN PSALM: THE WORKING CLASS

When I was seven
Years old, I remember one day
Looking out our big picture window

Seeing my grandfather pull up
In his late-1940s rusted-out
Dodge—stepping out with

His dented lunch bucket in hand.
And I wrote a poem in the margin
Of a second-grade textbook.

AMERICAN PSALM: AMERICAN ATHEISTS: A FRUIT AND TWO BUGS

First, I know you
Need the proof—hard
Evidence for sure. Well, here it is

Watermelon,
Beatles,
And the Infield Fly Rule.

All creations of God.
No human being in this dumb world
Could ever have created any of them.

AMERICAN PSALM: THE THANKSGIVING DINNER BLUES

Every year, the same old crap.
Uncle Gordy and Grandpa Stanley
Start their racist bitchin 'bout Welfare Queens.
Then it turns to Obama.

"That damn Kenyan!"
Uncle Gordy says. "I wants
My country back," and Grandpa screams
"I wants it back too!" but his dementia
Is advancing, so all he says is,

"Well, well, I sure as hell want something!"
I ask, "Grandpa, what is it you want?"
Then, he yells, "Just pass the mashed potatoes

And I'll have the white meat
Only—you smartass!"

AMERICAN PSALM: TEENAGE LUST

"LIFE COULD BE SO WONDERFUL"
THE RESIDENTS

When I turned from childhood
Into my early teen years, my friend
Dougy's dad married another
Neighbor friend's mother.

This was damn near heresy
In the early 1960s.
The neighbor's mother had
A beautiful daughter named
Norma. Her hair was golden

Blond and styled like Marianne
Faithfull's in Swinging London.
Straight. The cutest bangs
You'd ever seen. Since Dougy
Inherited a beautiful blond sister

From this sinister, much-whispered
About act of marriage, we asked
Dougy if he'd ever seen his gorgeous
Sister naked. He said adamantly,
"No!! You guys are gross." And we always

Said, "Dougy! Are you blind?" Still,
When I walk by Dougy
And Norma's old house, I imagine
Her fresh out of the shower and naked
Behind those blinds.

AMERICAN PSALM: THE LOW COST OF PUBLIC EDUCATION

When I was ten years old
And in the fifth grade, my teacher,
Mr. Wadkee, kept an old
Bus steering wheel
In our classroom.

Whenever kids acted up,
He made the hyper one
Sit in the front of the row
By the windows and hold
The old bus steering wheel.
He'd say, "Now you are
Driving the Stupid Bus!"

Most of the time
The same kid drove
The stupid bus. We'd howl,
Point, and giggle at the stupid kid.

Recently, I rode my bike
Through the old neighborhood,
And I noticed that the stupid kid
Lives in his parents' stupid old house.

I saw two vehicles parked there,
A pickup truck and a foreign car—
Of course—And both had "Piss
on Obama" decals on their back windows.

I'm going to a local junkyard
And buying an old steering wheel
And leaving it on his porch
On my next cycle through
The old neighborhood.

AMERICAN PSALM: AMERICAN HOUND DOG

"You Ain't Nothin But . . ."
Elvis was everything to me,
Because he was everything to my sweet grandmother.
Elvis was her cultural gift to me.
When a boy is four years old,
A character like Elvis is handsome,
larger than life and extremely cool.

His movie characters became my heroes.
I didn't watch cartoons;
I didn't listen to cute kiddie records on color vinyl
And grandma didn't read me no fairy tales
(Thank God, and screw the three bears).

Grandma never took me to the library
"Hound Dog" was my literature lesson,
"All Shook Up" became my politics,
"Love Me Tender" was my Shakespeare,
and "King Creole" was my *Moby-Dick.*

That was all pre-kindergarten,
and I loved it. Grandma loved that
I loved it!
And I truly loved her.

AMERICAN PSALM: AMERICAN BEATLE

FOR EMMITT RHODES

When I was seven years old in second grade,
My teacher wrote in the comments section
Of my report card, “Michael is an even-tempered boy,
But when provoked, his fists are soon flying.”

At eleven years old I heard,
“All You Need Is Love.”

And that changed everything!

AMERICAN PSALM: AMERICAN SILENCE

The door closing
When there is
No door.

AMERICAN PSALM: LIFE

Stay Alert—
You
Never
Know
Who
Will
Save yours.

ACKNOWLEDGMENTS

I would like to thank, with much deep gratitude, the good friends and wonderfully gifted poets who offered great editing suggestions and advice on this manuscript: Gary Metras, Maria Mazziotti Gillan, Barry Wallenstein. I am indebted to my wonderful team at Wayne State University Press who have helped me, supported me, and been extremely gracious and kind to me for many years: Annie Martin (of course), Emily Nowak (the best), Kristina Stonehill (my hometown girl), Jane Hoehner (director and Scholars' Day partner extraordinaire), Kathy Wildfong (who has been my press pal for a very long time), Jamie Jones (advertising manager), Bryce Schimanski (book designer supreme), Kristin Harpster (best book editor on planet Earth period), Gabe Gloden (the big lug), and Mike Delp (Bobsledding Champion of the Far North).

Of course, none of this would have been possible at all without my closest friend, confidant, and beautiful wife, Pam, who has stood by me since our early teen years beginning in 1969, or without our cool, hipster kids Shane and Shelby Liebler, who have provided me with more poetry and story fodder than imaginable over the past thirty-plus years.

Also, huge thanks to my heroes and friends who have been in my corner for a very long time: Michael Moore, Kathleen Glynn, Al Kooper, Mike Watt, Michael

Country Joe McDonald, Miriam and Ed Sanders, Joe Henry, Caroline Maun, Dave Marsh, Anca Vlasopolos, Melba Joyce Boyd, Jeff Ensroth, Carl Aniel, Gregory Hallock, Larry Wilson, Charlie Palazzola, Frankie the K, Ted Nagy, LouieDLou, Diane DeCillis, Bill and Carole Harris, Dean Western, Leonard Johnson, Thylias Moss, The Beardsley Family, Vanessa Lillian and Jorma Kaukonen, The Rev. Robert B. Jones, Eddie Baranek, Joel Martin, Scott Guy, Sean and Scott Forbes and families, Sarah Catlett and all of the staff at DPAN and 54 Sound, and to my late collaborators Faruq Z. Bey and Steve King, along with old pals and colleagues Phil Levine, Ken Kesey, Lawrence Pike, and Jayne Cortez, all of whom have carried the poetry beat forward into eternity.

I am extremely grateful for the generosity of Pauline Sutcliffe for letting me use her brother Stuart Sutcliffe's artwork for my cover. Stuart Sutcliffe was a Liverpool artist and musician best known as being the original bassist for The Beatles and John Lennon's closest friend. Sutcliffe left the band to pursue his career as an artist, having previously attended the Liverpool College of Art. He died in Hamburg, Germany, in 1962. I have been a fan of Stuart's art for a very long time. To view more of his artwork, go to www.stuartsutcliffeart.com

Finally a special thank you to Wayne State's Gloria Heppner (associate vice president for research) and her team for a 2014 Wayne State University President's Award in the Arts and Humanities, which helped greatly in the completion of this manuscript.

Many of the poems in this collection first appeared in *Paterson Literary Review*, *Passages North*, *LA Weekly*, *Orbis Quarterly International Literary Journal*, *Black Renaissance Noire*, *Newcity Chicago*, and Detroit's *Metro Times*.